Echoes

Megha Bammi

BookLeaf Publishing

India | USA | UK

Presentation by *BookLeaf Publishing*

Web: www.bookleafpub.com

E-mail: info@bookleafpub.com

ISBN: 9789360947880

First edition 2024

DEDICATION

This book is dedicated to my mother Deepty Bammi who always believed in my wildest dreams and supported my creative endeavors even when they seemed utterly absurd. To my partner Rohit Sharma who has made me laugh, made me cry, who inspired me and motivated me. Special thanks to my daughter Maisha, whose laughter and curiosity infuse my days with boundless joy and inspiration.

In memory of my father Late Chander Parkash Bammi who made me the person I am today.

To my friends, the wild and wonderful souls who have shared countless late nights of laughter and listened to my poems.

And to you, the one who holds this book in your hands, may these poems be your companion on the rollercoaster ride of life, offering solace, laughter, and maybe even a bit of magic.

ACKNOWLEDGEMENT

As I reflect on the completion of this poetry collection, I am overwhelmed with gratitude for the many individuals who have supported and inspired me along the way. First and foremost, I would like to express my deepest appreciation to my family for their unwavering love and encouragement. Your belief in me has been my guiding light through every step of this creative journey. To my friends, thank you for being my sounding board, my cheerleaders, and my sources of endless inspiration.

I am also grateful to the readers who have embraced my work and allowed my words to resonate with them. Your support means more to me than words can convey. Lastly, I would like to extend my appreciation to BookLeaf Publishing, who has helped me bring this project to fruition.

PREFACE

I started writing at the age of 16, but sadly I never preserved my poems, twenty-five years later I started again, with a husband and a 15-year-old daughter in my life. After an eventful life as a mother, wife, daughter etc, I turned 40 and decided to show some self-love. I took a vacation, spent some time with myself, the sun and the ocean. Soon after my thoughts started to pour on the notes app of my phone in the form of voices of my heart and my mind.

Welcome to "Echoes"— the little corner of the world where words dance and emotions run wild. This collection is like a mixtape of feelings, filled with love, laughs, and a few tears along the way. These poems are like whispers from the heart, bouncing around in my brain and finding their way onto these pages. Some are sweet like a Sunday morning, others hit you like a thunderstorm on a summer night, but all of them are pieces of me and you laid bare. So, kick back, grab your favourite blanket, and let's take a journey together. I hope you find a bit of yourself in these echoes, and maybe even a new perspective. Thanks for being part of this ride.

Hope

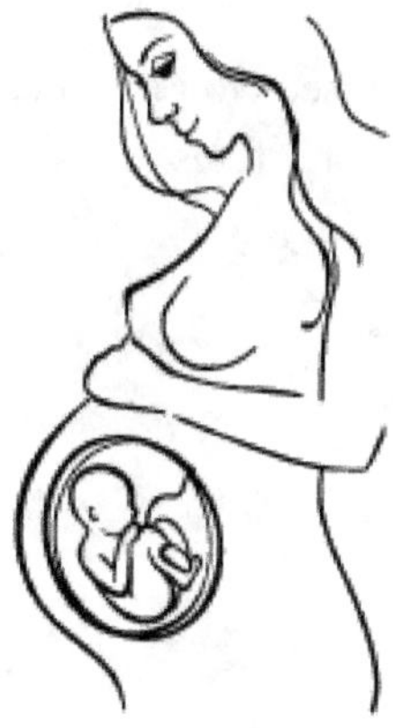

If hope had a face, it would be of a mother waiting for you to call.

If hope were some words, it would be what a father would say to his daughter's spouse.

Hope taking the shape of emotions will be a dog resting on the door for his owner.

Hope becomes a number when a poor starts counting his wage.

Walking on a journey is hope when your destination is faith.

Hope is to have seasons, days and nights, hope is to have years of sun and rain.

Hope for us is to see God in "Life after Death". Like it is Hope for a fetus to see its Mother in "Life After Delivery".

I Need

My Mom, who mends when I crack,
My Dad, who always has my back.
My teachers, who augment me bit by bit,
True friends, who tug & lug until it fits.
My dreams, which thrust me to the crown,
At last, it's me, who never lets me down.

Freedom

There is something in my hand, my dreams, my
wishes, and a friendship band.

Three colours of our flag, I see it stand tall on
my free land.

I can learn, play, demand my future,
my speech, my will, my freedom is my tutor.

I live in a free world, a free country and a free
community.
As our heroes, our leaders, our soldiers are on
duty.

Let us open our hands, set our dreams free,
And grow our freedom like a wise old banyan
tree.

My Valentine

A boy who helped me learn my ABCs,
who held my hand to jump over a puddle I didn't
see.
Love was smiling and drawing a straight line,
I was five, and I found a boy who was my
Valentine.

His eyes, his hair and the way he walked,
My first crush was a boy who never talked.
Love was admired and feelings were declined,
I was thirteen, and I found a boy who was my
Valentine.

He made me feel the beauty I always had,
He helped me fight the struggles when I was
mad.

Love was my first kiss and touch as we
intertwine,
I was sixteen, and I found a boy who was my
Valentine.

We planned our lives and built a house together,
He offered me his heart in exchange for my
feathers.
Love was devotion, patience, trust & timeline,
I was thirty and lived with a man who was my
Valentine.

He kissed, we danced, had fun on a starry night,
He appeared and disappeared at the onset of
daylight.
Love was the joy of self-love and getting fine
like wine,
I was near fifty, and I found myself to be my
Valentine.

He cooks and serves, does little chores around,
He reads as I look for glasses that are nowhere
to be found.
Love is being there to feel the affection that is
Devine,
I am nearly seventy, and I found us celebrating
our Valentine.

Unspoken

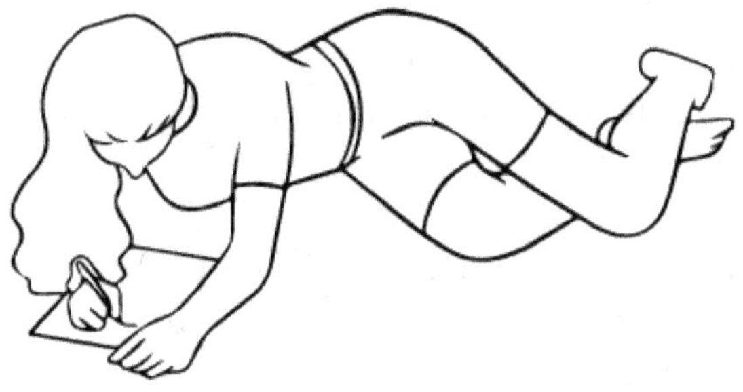

Some words unspoken, little notes and token.
White clouds of memories, pixy dust it carries.

How little it mentions, it seems intervention.
She wishes for more, random things and chores.

Like the kiss she got, the want she fought.
The peck on her cheek, makes her go weak.

Few doors to be opened, those eyes to be woken.
My heartbeat is dropping, someone's out still
knocking.

Deep down the layers, lies all her fears.
He's almost her fate, now the sleep has to wait.

They unite in shades, and the colours just fade.
They flow in a circle, make a mix of purple.

The music slows down, feels good to drown.
Her body fills with air, as light as her hair.

Smile mirrors in her eyes, in a beat, time flies.
It's all that she needs, for the passion to be freed.

Just then she returns, her soul still yearns.
Her dream is broken, the words are still
unspoken.

Unclichéd

It's not you or they, it's me that makes me happy.
It's not the sky and wind, it's being free that
makes me fly.

It's not what I read and learn, it's what I do that
makes me win.
It's not prayer and blessing, it's my deeds that
give me peace.

It's not what I buy and sell, it's what I give that
makes me wealthy.
It's not money and power, it's gratitude that
earns me respect.

It's not the salt and pepper, it's the flame that
cooks my food.
It's not milk and cookies, it's my mate who
helps me grow.

It's not love and nookie, it's the friendship that
makes us last.
It's not when I worry, it's when I am poised that
solves the case.

It's not water and soil, it's what I sow, I get to
reap.
It's not the Sun and moon, it's your smile that
makes my day.

The Night

I feel just everything to him.

A friend, a crush, a companion, and a rush.
Smiling, laughing, giggling, jumping up &
down.
A guide, a flight, a halt and a beautiful sight.
Thinking, comparing, wanting, allowing &
owning.
All of this and much more on a whim,
I feel just everything to him.

I feel just nothing to him

A night, a moment, a song and a sense.
A thought, a desire, a phase and a fence.

Waiting, planning, sorting, making it right
A girl, a name, a person, a glim
I feel just nothing to him.

He feels just everything to me

A friend, a crush, a companion, and a rush.
Talking, listening, wondering, loving & caring.
A craze, a breeze, a flame, and a crown.
Juggling, steering, patting & kneading.
All and much more that I can't see,
he feels just everything to me

He feels just nothing to me

A drink, a dance, a hand & a stare.
A party, a place, the time & some fear.
Walking, stopping, looking and shuddering.
A boy that night with an impish glee
he feels just nothing to me.

Theatre

I want to write a song or a story,
That plots around your anger, love & glory.

The melody of a natter that brings a smile to me,
Some scenes of you smiling that I long to see.

I sing & narrate to the tune of your beat.
When I look into your eyes, I often want to
cheat.

I will plot a romance that has no tragic end.
I'll turn the love to good-will so that it can fend.

I dance with the sway as you move your feet on
the floor.
This tale will not end until someone knocks on
the door.

I'll script all I fancy and the warmth I can give,
"It was only in the theater that I lived". (-Oscar
Wilde-)

My List

I need a bucket list for my imaginary life in a
gist.

A visit to the streets of London, drinking coffee
& eating brownies in dozen.

Walking with him in the cold weather, our warm
hands that are held together.

Looking into his eyes to find myself, in a place
decorated with deer & elves.

Losing touch with time while I open my heart,
sipping few drinks in a Bar with a game of dart.

To look into the mirror and cherish what I see, I
wish to see you, standing with me.

Not just chilly evenings, to spend some warmer
days too, babble about the past year, while
having a fondue.

To sit with my feet dipped into the warm beach,
soaking the sun and the waves beyond my reach.

I have a to-do list for whenever I'll get to see
you, to adore, admire and cherish all that is due.

Birthday Card

How do I express my love and gratitude for one
who gave my words power again?
To tell you how I feel is odd, I met you and
started to feel again.

I don't know how I name you, you gave my
name meaning again,
Do I say it aloud? Like how you made my voice
heard again.

Do I use some adjectives to describe you? as
now I have them in my life again,
Maybe just sketch your face on a paper, for you
gave me ink and colour again.

Can I just narrate how I see you in my dreams?
as I have lots of dreams again.

Rather explain the way you smile, for you made
me smile again.

What I like in you is of no relevance now, as you
made me relevant again,
I give you my unexpressed emotions, as I learnt
to start giving again.

I have no words for you, but I grew, I stretched,
and I am ecstatic with you again.
I wish the Sun and moon for you, for now, they
are my friends again.

It's a Date

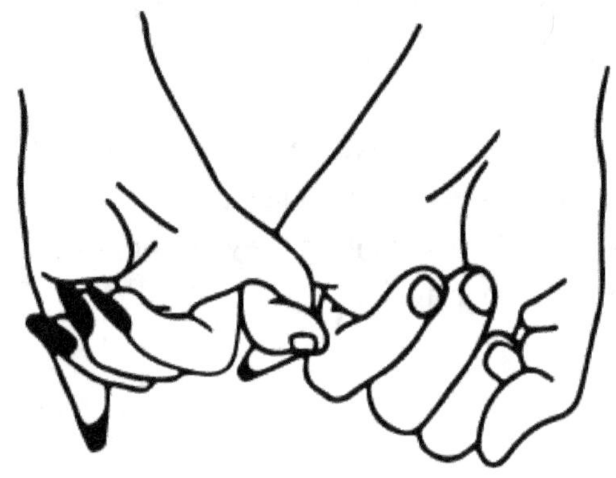

I get on the road, walking while my heart is
racing.
I grab my thoughts, collect my words, and some
air that's bracing.

I wonder what and when? Should he, or I should
touch?
I see him across the street, I pause my mind and
find something to clutch.

The food is nice, and the wine glides right into
my senses.
The guards are down, as we talk. I watch him
cross the fences.

I walk with him, gently feeling the air that
surrounds him.
Neither feeling the ground, nor I am aware of
my limb.

I played what I rehearsed, now I'm short of what
is next.
I will let him take the lead, the move, the place
and the rest.

A million times I rolled it, felt it, and desired it
to be my date.
I smiled and knew it was a fantasy, as I was
getting late.

We'll make her again

You and me walking and falling, finding our way to love.
From days to weeks and then to years, fitting into one glove.

We tied the knot on a sunny day spreading laughter, light and joy.
Our loved ones blessed us with their golden hearts, said "You should soon get a toy".

With summer glazing right on our faces, we felt
the warmth, wrapped in a shade.
Soon our hearts were linked up with a chord, the
tender, soft child we have made.

Our world was filled with some fresh new
sounds that jingled all the time.
Least we knew the sweet day and night was
turning as sour as lime.

We cried, we screamed, we fought, we broke
and were angry with our god.
We stood, we smiled, we worked, we prayed and
continued to trod.

In the gloomy rains with a cloudy sky, we trying
to relieve ourselves of pain.
Now the time has come for you and me to
nurture and grow her again.

Her smile will help, and her eyes will help, when
she rises after every fall.
Not you, not me, the one amongst three, it's she
who's bravest of all.

Our strength, our faith, our joy and our life,
there's lots we need to regain.

Last year we made a beautiful being, now together "WE'LL MAKE HER AGAIN".

"To whom it may concern"

All the nights that have not seen the dreams,
Heart full of dry tears and lots of unheard
screams.

In denial, falling out of love with hoping to fall
back again,
Skin is turning cold & pale, with red turning into
blue veins.

Every push and every fall scrubbing me smaller,
What once was beauty infinite is now a mere
crawler.

My soul & face are not mine anymore,
Even my shadow hides in and stands at the door.

My desires have no mass, no volume, no use.
To find a little joy, I have to look for clues.

What face I wear is a sham you believe,
Not to myself but there is something you
achieve.

I dash through the darkness with the injuries I
have borne,
Towards the brightness in light picking every
thorne.

"I miss you"

I miss you, not for the time we spend together. It's moments and some conversation that we built. I miss what we make.

It's not the attention that you give me, and it's not it that I look for. I miss the person I become when I am talking to you.

You don't make me feel beautiful, as that's something I know I am. It's the beauty of my soul that I can see from your eyes that I miss.

I just don't miss the song that reminds me of you, it's what I felt in your presence that made the song special.

I can just say "I miss you". but that's not just what I do. It's the memories I create that I miss too.

Sailor

Me and my daughter stand by the bank and stare
at the sea.
I tell her, it made me the hero you see in me.

It was harsh to me but I stood by every tide and
storm.
It hit my boat on every side but the water
splashed on me was warm.

My queens on water bore struggles with me in
trade for some fresh paint.
I had them in vibrant colours but my last queen
was white and quaint.

My little girl proudly said, "I love the sea", it's
fresh and cold.
I held her hand to guard her from the waves and
see my life unfold.

Good morning Cap! Copy that Cap! How to do
this Cap! Everyone is in vain.
And me, the Cap! has always said "Did
everyone see that? Because I will not be doing it
again."

Now the sea has succumbed, my queens are
proud and my sub has learnt it all.
"Vessel Anchored", is my final command as the
anchor falls and I stand tall.

To all the nights and all the days, my question as
a sailor from dusk to dawn.
I ask my mates at the end of this "Why is the
rum gone?" (-Captain Jack Sparrow-)

Boundaries

I owe you, not some words or a smile,
I owe that we have not spoken in a while.

I owe you, not my life that I can't share.
I owe to say it more that I am there.

I owe you, not to return favours I got,
I owe the gratitude for loving me at my worst.

I owe you, not to be the way you want,
I owe to be the man who no more haunts.

I owe you, not to please desires in you,
I owe to say all that I admire in you.

I owe you, not to feed into your spite.
I owe to regard the courage you gave me to
fight.

I owe you, not to give you all that you gave me,
I owe to accept that you and me cannot be we.

Time

Time that needed me to caress it, so it absorbs the sorrows and cushions only joy.

Time when I held lives in my arms, now I am still there, holding nothing but their toy.

Time was beautiful, walking by me, taking me to the place of my dreams. I am still walking, unaware of the destination that I might enjoy.

Time tells me thousand stories to calm me down and make me smile. But I am still waiting to listen to the truth of my heart, the one that is destroyed.

Time allowed me to freeze those moments when
I had no reason to write, I stand shocked! not
surprised, for now, I need some soldiers to
deploy.

Time I spent in some ancient years that
accumulated me a bag of "karma". I move in
circles, wondering what it is that I cloy.

Time has never given me a start, I just caught it
in the middle somewhere. I accepted all that
came my way, only to see at the end that it was a
decoy.

Time will keep wheeling till eternity, it never
had me forever. While walking on sand and
pebbles, sometime at dusk I'll stop and coil.

I win

I doubt my every move and every play,
Working harder, getting ready to slay.

One of the many, but not the best of all,
What I have is the flair for rising after each fall.

My eye is on the trophy and my mind is on the
task
Yes! I am a winner, an achiever if you may ask.

I've always learnt to race, to leave rest behind,
To get fierce in my game, so forget being kind.

I am only feeding my brain, my body lacks
wealth,
Spending hour by hour in haste, plunging into
depth.

My motto is to thrive, stepping on every stone
and pebble.
The ride appears to dwindle, as I reach for the
medal.

My mentor gives me a jiggle and asks me the
cause.
I am caught up in the rally, why take a pause?

So, I am told that the trophy will find a new
hero.
And the medal will fade, leaving me with my
ego.

Today I give you a lesson on the story of my
success,
My goals, learnings, and findings, that I have to
confess.

I ran very fast, starving myself of even water,

The nights were colder as the days became
hotter.

I did reach the top, with gold and fame in my
pocket,
I was left alone on my way, who said it's easy to
earn profit.

I used my wit, grit, and labour, put my life on a
spin,
It is not the victory, but the failure that made me
win.